DREAM
WORK

DREAM WORK

*Mary
Oliver*

THE ATLANTIC MONTHLY PRESS
NEW YORK
♦

Published simultaneously in Canada
Printed in the United States of America

Library of Congress Cataloging-in-Publication Data

Oliver, Mary, 1935–
    Dream work.

    I. Title
PS3565.L5D74   1986   811'.54   86-7656
ISBN: 978-0-87113-069-3

Design by Dede Cummings

Atlantic Monthly Press
an imprint of Grove/Atlantic, Inc.
841 Broadway
New York, NY 10003

Distributed by Publishers Group West

www.groveatlantic.com

10 11 12 13 14   30 29 28 27 26 25

～ CONTENTS

I

∽ DOGFISH

Some kind of relaxed and beautiful thing
kept flickering in with the tide
and looking around.
Black as a fisherman's boot,
with a white belly.

If you asked for a picture I would have to draw a smile
under the perfectly round eyes and above the chin,
which was rough
as a thousand sharpened nails.

And you know
what a smile means,
don't you?

∽

I wanted
the past to go away, I wanted
to leave it, like another country; I wanted
my life to close, and open
like a hinge, like a wing, like the part of the song
     where it falls
down over the rocks: an explosion, a discovery;
     I wanted
to hurry into the work of my life; I wanted to know,

whoever I was, I was

alive
for a little while.

❧

It was evening, and no longer summer.
Three small fish, I don't know what they were,
huddled in the highest ripples
as it came swimming in again, effortless, the whole body
one gesture, one black sleeve
that could fit easily around
the bodies of three small fish.

❧

Also I wanted
to be able to love. And we all know
how that one goes,
don't we?

Slowly

❧

the dogfish tore open the soft basins of water.

❧

You don't want to hear the story
of my life, and anyway
I don't want to tell it, I want to listen

to the enormous waterfalls of the sun.

And anyway it's the same old story —
a few people just trying,
one way or another,
to survive.

Mostly, I want to be kind.
And nobody, of course, is kind,
or mean,
for a simple reason.

And nobody gets out of it, having to
swim through the fires to stay in
this world.

❧

And look! look! look! I think those little fish
better wake up and dash themselves away
from the hopeless future that is
bulging toward them.

❧

And probably,
if they don't waste time
looking for an easier world,

they can do it.

∿ MORNING POEM

Every morning
the world
is created.
Under the orange

sticks of the sun
the heaped
ashes of the night
turn into leaves again

and fasten themselves to the high branches —
and the ponds appear
like black cloth
on which are painted islands

of summer lilies.
If it is your nature
to be happy
you will swim away along the soft trails

for hours, your imagination
alighting everywhere.
And if your spirit
carries within it

the thorn
that is heavier than lead —
if it's all you can do
to keep on trudging —

there is still
somewhere deep within you
a beast shouting that the earth
is exactly what it wanted —

each pond with its blazing lilies
is a prayer heard and answered
lavishly,
every morning,

whether or not
you have ever dared to be happy,
whether or not
you have ever dared to pray.

∿ THE CHANCE TO LOVE EVERYTHING

All summer I made friends
with the creatures nearby —
they flowed through the fields
and under the tent walls,
or padded through the door,
grinning through their many teeth,
looking for seeds,
suet, sugar; mutttering and humming,
opening the breadbox, happiest when
there was milk and music. But once
in the night I heard a sound
outside the door, the canvas
bulged slightly — something
was pressing inward at eye level.
I watched, trembling, sure I had heard
the click of claws, the smack of lips
outside my gauzy house —
I imagined the red eyes,
the broad tongue, the enormous lap.
Would it be friendly too?
Fear defeated me. And yet,
not in faith and not in madness
but with the courage I thought
my dream deserved,
I stepped outside. It was gone.
Then I whirled at the sound of some
shambling tonnage.
Did I see a black haunch slipping
back through the trees? Did I see

the moonlight shining on it?
Did I actually reach out my arms
toward it, toward paradise falling, like
the fading of the dearest, wildest hope —
the dark heart of the story that is all
the reason for its telling?

∽ TRILLIUMS

Every spring
  among
    the ambiguities
    of childhood

the hillsides grew white
  with the wild trilliums.
    I believed in the world.
    Oh, I wanted

to be easy
  in the peopled kingdoms,
    to take my place there,
    but there was none

that I could find
  shaped like me.
    So I entered
    through the tender buds,

I crossed the cold creek,
  my backbone
    and my thin white shoulders
    unfolding and stretching.

From the time of snow-melt,
  when the creek roared
    and the mud slid
    and the seeds cracked,

I listened to the earth-talk,
  the root-wrangle,
    the arguments of **energy**,
      the dreams lying

just under the surface,
  then rising,
    becoming
      at the last moment

flaring and luminous —
  the patient parable
    of every spring and hillside
      year after difficult year.

～ RAGE

You are the dark song
of the morning;
serious and slow,
you shave, you dress,
you descend the stairs
in your public clothes
and drive away, you become
the wise and powerful one
who makes all the days
possible in the world.
But you were also the red song
in the night,
stumbling through the house
to the child's bed,
to the damp rose of her body,
leaving your bitter taste.
And forever those nights snarl
the delicate machinery of the days.
When the child's mother smiles
you see on her cheekbones
a truth you will never confess;
and you see how the child grows —
timidly, crouching in corners.
Sometimes in the wide night
you hear the most mournful cry,
a ravished and terrible moment.
In your dreams she's a tree
that will never come to leaf —

in your dreams she's a watch
you dropped on the dark stones
till no one could gather the fragments —
in your dreams you have sullied and murdered,
and dreams do not lie.

∿ WILD GEESE

You do not have to be good.
You do not have to walk on your knees
for a hundred miles through the desert, repenting.
You only have to let the soft animal of your body
   love what it loves.
Tell me about despair, yours, and I will tell you mine.
Meanwhile the world goes on.
Meanwhile the sun and the clear pebbles of the rain
are moving across the landscapes,
over the prairies and the deep trees,
the mountains and the rivers.
Meanwhile the wild geese, high in the clean blue air,
are heading home again.
Whoever you are, no matter how lonely,
the world offers itself to your imagination,
calls to you like the wild geese, harsh and exciting —
over and over announcing your place
in the family of things.

∽ KNIFE

Something
just now
moved through my heart
like the thinnest of blades
as that red-tail pumped
once with its great wings
and flew above the gray, cracked
rock wall.
It wasn't
about the bird, it was
something about the way
stone stays
mute and put, whatever
goes flashing by.
Sometimes,
when I sit like this, quiet,
all the dreams of my blood
and all outrageous divisions of time
seem ready to leave,
to slide out of me.
Then, I imagine, I would never move.
By now
the hawk has flown five miles
at least,
dazzling whoever else has happened
to look up.
I was dazzled. But that
wasn't the knife.
It was the sheer, dense wall

of blind stone
without a pinch of hope
or a single unfulfilled desire
sponging up and reflecting,
so brilliantly,
as it has for centuries,
the sun's fire.

∽ SHADOWS

Everyone knows the great energies running amok cast
terrible shadows, that each of the so-called
senseless acts has its thread looping
back through the world and into a human heart.
        And meanwhile
the gold-trimmed thunder
wanders the sky; the river
may be filling the cellars of the sleeping town.
Cyclone, fire, and their merry cousins
        bring us to grief — but these are the hours
with the old wooden-god faces;
we lift them to our shoulders like so many
black coffins, we continue walking
into the future. I don't mean
        there are no bodies in the river,
or bones broken by the wind. I mean
everyone who has heard the lethal train-roar
of the tornado swears there was no mention ever
of any person, or reason — I mean
        the waters rise without any plot upon
history, or even geography. Whatever
power of the earth rampages, we turn to it
dazed but anonymous eyes; whatever
the name of the catastrophe, it is never
        the opposite of love.

∽ DREAMS

All night
the dark buds of dreams
open
richly.

In the center
of every petal
is a letter,
and you imagine

if you could only remember
and string them all together
they would spell the answer.
It is a long night,

and not an easy one —
you have so many branches,
and there are diversions —
birds that come and go,

the black fox that lies down
to sleep beneath you,
the moon staring
with her bone-white eye.

Finally you have spent
all the energy you can
and you drag from the ground
the muddy skirt of your roots

and leap awake
with two or three syllables
like water in your mouth
and a sense

of loss — a memory
not yet of a word,
certainly not yet the answer —
only how it feels

when deep in the tree
all the locks click open,
and the fire surges through the wood,
and the blossoms blossom.

∽ THE RIVER

In one day the Amazon discharges into the Atlantic the
equivalent of New York City's water supply for nine years.
— *New York Times*

Just because I was born
precisely here or there,
in some cold city or other,
don't think I don't remember
how I came along like a grain
carried by the flood

on one of the weedy threads that pour
toward a muddy lightning,
surging east, past
monkeys and parrots, past
trees with their branches in the clouds, until
I was spilled forth

and slept under the blue lung
of the Caribbean.

Nobody
told me this. But little by little
the smell of mud and leaves returned to me,
and in dreams I began to turn,
to sense the current.

Do dreams lie? Once I was a fish
crying for my sisters in the sprawling

crossroads of the delta.
Once among the reeds I found
a boat, as thin and lonely
as a young tree. Nearby
the forest sizzled with the afternoon rain.

Home, I said.
In every language there is a word for it.
In the body itself, climbing
those walls of white thunder, past those green
temples, there is also
a word for it.
I said, home.

∼ CONSEQUENCES

Afterward
I found under my left shoulder
the most curious wound.
As though I had leaned against
some whirring thing,
it bleeds secretly.
Nobody knows its name.

Afterward,
for a reason more right than rational,
I thought of that fat German
in his ill-fitting overcoat
in the woods near Vienna, realizing
that the birds were going farther and farther away, and
no matter how fast he walked
he couldn't keep up.

How does any of us live in this world?
One thing compensates for another, I suppose.
Sometimes what's wrong does not hurt at all, but rather
shines like a new moon.

I often think of Beethoven
rising, when he couldn't sleep,
stumbling through the dust and crumpled papers,
yawning, settling at the piano,
inking in rapidly note after note after note.

∼ ROBERT SCHUMANN

Hardly a day passes I don't think of him
in the asylum: younger

than I am now, trudging the long road down
through madness toward death.

Everywhere in this world his music
explodes out of itself, as he

could not. And now I understand
something so frightening, and wonderful —

how the mind clings to the road it knows, rushing
through crossroads, sticking

like lint to the familiar. So!
Hardly a day passes I don't

think of him: nineteen, say, and it is
spring in Germany

and he has just met a girl named Clara.
He turns the corner,

he scrapes the dirt from his soles,
he runs up the dark staircase, humming.

✎ CLAMMING

I rise
by lamplight and hurry out
to the bay
where the gulls like white

ghosts swim
in the shallows —
I rake and rake
down to the gray stones,

the clenched quahogs,
the deadweight
fruits of the sea that bear
inside their walls

a pink and salty
one-lunged life;
we are all
one family

but love ourselves
best. Later I sit
on the dawn-soaked shore and set
a thin blade

into the slightly
hissing space between
the shells and slash through
the crisp life-muscle; I put

what is in the shell
into my mouth, and when
the gulls come begging
I feed them too.

How detailed and hopeful,
how exact
everything is in the light,
on the rippling sand,

at the edge of the turning tide —
its upheaval —
its stunning proposal —
its black, anonymous roar.

∽ THE FIRE

That winter it seemed the city
was always burning — night after night
the flames leaped, the ladders pitched forward.
Scorched but alive, the homeless wailed
    as they ran for the cold streets.
That winter my mind had turned around,
shedding, like leaves, its bolts of information —
drilling down, through history,
toward my motionless heart.
    Those days I was willing, but frightened.
What I mean is, I wanted to live my life
but I didn't want to do what I had to do
to go on, which was: to go back.
All winter the fires kept burning,
    the smoke swirled, the flames grew hotter.
I began to curse, to stumble and choke.
Everything, solemnly, drove me toward it —
the crying out, that's so hard to do.
Then over my head the red timbers floated,
    my feet were slippers of fire, my voice
crashed at the truth, my fists
smashed at the flames to find the door —
wicked and sad, mortal and bearable,
    it fell open forever as I burned.

~ BANYAN

Something screamed
from the fringes of the swamp.
It was Banyan,
the old merchant.

It was the hundred-legged
tree, walking again.

The cattle egrets
flew out into the sunlight
like so many pieces of white ribbon.

The watersnakes slipped down the banks
like green hooks and floated away.

Banyan groaned.
A knee down in the east corner buckled,

a gray shin rose, and the root,
wet and hairy,
sank back in, a little closer.

Then a voice like a howling wind deep in the leaves said:
I'll tell you a story
about a seed.

About a seed flying into a tree, and eating it
little by little.

About a small tree that becomes a huge tree
and wants to travel.

Listen, said the voice.
This is your dream.

I'm only stopping here for a little while.
Don't be afraid.

∿ WHISPERS

Have you ever
tried to
slide into
the heaven of sensation and met

you know not what
resistance but it
held you back? have you ever
turned on your shoulder

helplessly, facing
the white moon, crying
let me in? have you dared to count
the months as they pass and the years

while you imagined pleasure,
shining like honey, locked in some
secret tree? have you dared to feel
the isolation gathering

intolerably and recognized
what kinds of explosions can follow
from an intolerable condition? have you
walked out in the mornings

wherever you are in the world to consider
all those gleaming and reasonless lives
that flow outward and outward, easily, to the last
moment the bulbs of their lungs,

their bones and their appetites,
can carry them? oh, have you
looked wistfully into
the flushed bodies of the flowers? have you stood,

staring out over the swamps, the swirling rivers
where the birds like tossing fires
flash through the trees, their bodies
exchanging a certain happiness

in the sleek, amazing
humdrum of nature's design —
blood's heaven, spirit's haven, to which
you cannot belong?

∽ DRIVING THROUGH THE WIND RIVER RESERVATION: A POEM OF BLACK BEAR

In the time of snow, in the time of sleep.
The rivers themselves changed into links
of white iron, holding everything. Once
she woke deep in the leaves under
the fallen tree and peered
through the loose bark and saw him:
a tall white bone
with thick shoulders, like a wrestler,
roaring the saw-toothed music
of wind and sleet, legs pumping
up and down the hills.
Well, she thought, he'll wear himself out
running around like that.
She slept again
while he drove on through the trees,
snapping off the cold pines, gasping,
rearranging over and over
the enormous drifts. Finally one morning
the sun rose up like a pot of blood
and his knees buckled.
Well, she whispered from the leaves,
that's that. In the distance
the ice began to boom and wrinkle
and a dampness
that could not be defeated began
to come from her, her breathing
enlarged, oh, tender mountain, she rearranged
herself so that the cubs
could slide from her body, so that the rivers
would flow.

∾ MEMBERS OF THE TRIBE

Ahead of me
they were lighting their fires
in the dark forests
of death.

Should I name them?
Their names make a long branch of sound.

You know them.

∾

I know
death is the fascinating snake
under the leaves, sliding
and sliding; I know
the heart loves him too, can't
turn away, can't

break the spell. Everything

wants to enter the slow thickness,
aches to be peaceful finally and at any cost.

Wants to be stone.

∾

That time
I wanted to die
somebody
was playing the piano
in the room with me.

It was Mozart.
It was Beethoven.
It was Bruckner.

In the kitchen
a man with one ear
was painting a flower.

❧

Later,
in the asylum,
I began to pick through the red rivers
of confusion;

I began to take apart
the deep stitches
of nightmares.

This was good, human work.

This had nothing to do with laying down a path of words
that could throttle,
or soften,
the human heart.

Meanwhile,
Yeats, in love and anger,
stood beside his fallen friends;
Whitman kept falling
through the sleeve of ego.

In the back fields,
beyond the locked windows,
a young man who couldn't live long and knew it
was listening to a plain brown bird
that kept singing in the deep leaves,
that kept urging from him
some wild and careful words.
                              You know that
important and eloquent defense
of sanity.

                    ❧

I forgive them
their unhappiness,
I forgive them
for walking out of the world.

But I don't forgive them
for turning their faces away,
for taking off their veils
and dancing for death —

for hurtling
toward oblivion
on the sharp blades
of their exquisite poems, saying:
this is the way.

                    ❧

I was, of course, all that time
coming along
behind them, and listening
for advice.

∽

And the man who merely
washed Michelangelo's brushes, kneeling
on the damp bricks, staring
every day at the colors pouring out of them,

lived to be a hundred years old.

∽ STARFISH

In the sea rocks,
　　in the stone pockets
　　　　under the tide's lip,
　　　　　　in water dense as blindness

they slid
　　like sponges,
　　　　like too many thumbs.
　　　　　　I knew this, and what I wanted

was to draw my hands back
　　from the water — what I wanted
　　　　was to be willing
　　　　　　to be afraid.

But I stayed there,
　　I crouched on the stone wall
　　　　while the sea poured its harsh song
　　　　　　through the sluices,

while I waited for the gritty lightning
　　of their touch, while I stared
　　　　down through the tide's leaving
　　　　　　where sometimes I could see them —

their stubborn flesh
　　lounging on my knuckles.
　　　　What good does it do
　　　　　　to lie all day in the sun

loving what is easy?
   It never grew easy,
      but at last I grew peaceful:
         all summer

my fear diminished
   as they bloomed through the water
      like flowers, like flecks
         of an uncertain dream,

while I lay on the rocks, reaching
   into the darkness, learning
      little by little to love
         our only world.

∿ THE JOURNEY

One day you finally knew
what you had to do, and began,
though the voices around you
kept shouting
their bad advice —
though the whole house
began to tremble
and you felt the old tug
at your ankles.
"Mend my life!"
each voice cried.
But you didn't stop.
You knew what you had to do,
though the wind pried
with its stiff fingers
at the very foundations —
though their melancholy
was terrible.
It was already late
enough, and a wild night,
and the road full of fallen
branches and stones.
But little by little,
as you left their voices behind,
the stars began to burn
through the sheets of clouds,
and there was a new voice,
which you slowly
recognized as your own,

that kept you company
as you strode deeper and deeper
into the world,
determined to do
the only thing you could do —
determined to save
the only life you could save.

∽ A VISITOR

My father, for example,
who was young once
and blue-eyed,
returns
on the darkest of nights
to the porch and knocks
wildly at the door,
and if I answer
I must be prepared
for his waxy face,
for his lower lip
swollen with bitterness.
And so, for a long time,
I did not answer,
but slept fitfully
between his hours of rapping.
But finally there came the night
when I rose out of my sheets
and stumbled down the hall.
The door fell open

and I knew I was saved
and could bear him,
pathetic and hollow,
with even the least of his dreams
frozen inside him,
and the meanness gone.
And I greeted him and asked him
into the house,

and lit the lamp,
and looked into his blank eyes
in which at last
I saw what a child must love,
I saw what love might have done
had we loved in time.

∿ THE HOUSE

It grows larger,
wall after wall
sliding
on some miraculous arrangement
of panels,
blond and weightless
as balsa, making space
for windows, alcoves,
more rooms, stairways
and passages, all
bathed
in light, with here
and there the green
flower of a tree,
vines, streams
casually
breaking through —
what a change
from the cramped
room at the center
where I began, where I crouched
and was safe, but could hardly
breathe! Day after day
I labor at it;
night after night
I keep going —
I'm clearing new ground,
I'm lugging boards,
I'm measuring,

I'm hanging sheets of glass,
I'm nailing down the hardwoods,
the thresholds —
I'm hinging the doors —
once they are up they will lift
their easy latches, they will open
like wings.

∾ STANLEY KUNITZ

I used to imagine him
coming from the house, like Merlin
strolling with important gestures
through the garden
where everything grows so thickly,
where birds sing, little snakes lie
on the boughs, thinking of nothing
but their own good lives,
where petals float upward,
their colors exploding,
and trees open their moist
pages of thunder —
it has happened every summer for years.

But now I know more
about the great wheel of growth,
and decay, and rebirth,
and know my vision for a falsehood.
Now I see him coming from the house —
I see him on his knees,
cutting away the diseased, the superfluous,
coaxing the new,
knowing that the hour of fulfillment
is buried in years of patience —
yet willing to labor like that
on the mortal wheel.

Oh, what good it does the heart
to know it isn't magic!
Like the human child I am
I rush to imitate —
I watch him as he bends
among the leaves and vines
to hook some weed or other;
even when I do not see him,
I think of him there
raking and trimming, stirring up
those sheets of fire
between the smothering weights of earth,
the wild and shapeless air.

~ II ~

∽ ORION

I love Orion, his fiery body, his ten stars,
his flaring points of reference, his shining dogs.
"It is winter," he says.
"We must eat," he says. Our gloomy
and passionate teacher.
                              Miles below
in the cold woods, with the mouse and the owl,
with the clearness of water sheeted and hidden,
with the reason for the wind forever a secret,
he descends and sits with me, his voice
like the snapping of bones.
                              Behind him
everything is so black and unclassical; behind him
I don't know anything, not even
my own mind.

∽ ONE OR TWO THINGS

1

Don't bother me.
I've just
been born.

2

The butterfly's loping flight
carries it through the country of the leaves
delicately, and well enough to get it
where it wants to go, wherever that is, stopping
here and there to fuzzle the damp throats
of flowers and the black mud; up
and down it swings, frenzied and aimless; and sometimes

for long delicious moments it is perfectly
lazy, riding motionless in the breeze on the soft stalk
of some ordinary flower.

3

The god of dirt
came up to me many times and said
so many wise and delectable things, I lay
on the grass listening
to his dog voice,
crow voice,
frog voice; *now*,
he said, and *now*,

and never once mentioned *forever*,

4

which has nevertheless always been,
like a sharp iron hoof,
at the center of my mind.

5

One or two things are all you need
to travel over the blue pond, over the deep
roughage of the trees and through the stiff
flowers of lightning — some deep
memory of pleasure, some cutting
knowledge of pain.

6

But to lift the hoof!
For that you need
an idea.

7

For years and years I struggled
just to love my life. And then

the butterfly
rose, weightless, in the wind.
"Don't love your life
too much," it said,

and vanished
into the world.

∿ POEM

The spirit
   likes to dress up like this:
      ten fingers,
        ten toes,

shoulders, and all the rest
   at night
      in the black branches,
        in the morning

in the blue branches
   of the world.
      It could float, of course,
        but would rather

plumb rough matter.
   Airy and shapeless thing,
      it needs
        the metaphor of the body,

lime and appetite,
   the oceanic fluids;
      it needs the body's world,
        instinct

and imagination
   and the dark hug of time,
      sweetness
        and tangibility,

to be understood,
   to be more than pure light
      that burns
         where no one is —

so it enters us —
   in the morning
      shines from brute comfort
         like a stitch of lightning;

and at night
   lights up the deep and wondrous
      drownings of the body
         like a star.

∿ MARSH HAWKS

In the morning they glide
just above the rough plush
of the marshlands,
as though on leashes,
long-tailed and with
yard-wide wings
tipped upward, like
dark Vs; then they suddenly fall
in response to their wish,
which is always the same —
to succeed again and again.
What they eat
is neither fruit nor grain,
what they cry out
is sharper than a sharp word.
At night they don't exist, except
in our dreams, where they fly
like mad things, unleashed
and endlessly hungry.
But in the day
they are always there gliding
and when they descend to the marsh
they are swift, and then so quiet
they could be anything —
a rock, an uprise of earth,
a scrap of fallen tree,
a patch of flowers
casting their whirling shadow.

∽ BOWING TO THE EMPRESS

Through the forest,
through the branches
of shagbarks and walnuts,
through the feathers
of the February snow,
she flows
to her nest
of a thousand
broken and braided sticks,
to her chicks
yelping like tiny wolves,
like downy
emperors for her return,
for her attention,
for red meat,
and you know
theirs is a decent task
in the scheme of things —
the hunters,
the rapacious
plucking up the timid
like so many soft jewels.
They are what keeps everything
enough, but not too many —
and so you bow
to the lightning of her eyes,
the pick of her beak,
the swale of her appetite,

and even to her shadow
over the field — when it passes
you can hardly breathe,
the world is that bright,
your senses so sharply tuned
by the notion of oblivion —
those black wings beating
at the light.

✧ THE TURTLE

breaks from the blue-black
skin of the water, dragging her shell
with its mossy scutes
across the shallows and through the rushes
and over the mudflats, to the uprise,
to the yellow sand,
to dig with her ungainly feet
a nest, and hunker there spewing
her white eggs down
into the darkness, and you think

of her patience, her fortitude,
her determination to complete
what she was born to do —
and then you realize a greater thing —
she doesn't consider
what she was born to do.
She's only filled
with an old blind wish.
It isn't even hers but came to her
in the rain or the soft wind,
which is a gate through which her life keeps walking.

She can't see
herself apart from the rest of the world
or the world from what she must do
every spring.
Crawling up the high hill,

luminous under the sand that has packed against her skin,
she doesn't dream,
she knows

she is a part of the pond she lives in,
the tall trees are her children,
the birds that swim above her
are tied to her by an unbreakable string.

∽ SUNRISE

You can
die for it —
an idea,
or the world. People

have done so,
brilliantly,
letting
their small bodies be bound

to the stake,
creating
an unforgettable
fury of light. But

this morning,
climbing the familiar hills
in the familiar
fabric of dawn, I thought

of China,
and India
and Europe, and I thought
how the sun

blazes
for everyone just
so joyfully
as it rises

under the lashes
of my own eyes, and I thought
I am so many!
What is my name?

What is the name
of the deep breath I would take
over and over
for all of us? Call it

whatever you want, it is
happiness, it is another one
of the ways to enter
fire.

∽ TWO KINDS OF DELIVERANCE

1

Last night the geese came back,
slanting fast
from the blossom of the rising moon down
to the black pond. A muskrat
swimming in the twilight saw them and hurried

to the secret lodges to tell everyone
spring had come.

And so it had.
By morning when I went out
the last of the ice had disappeared, blackbirds
sang on the shores. Every year
the geese, returning,
do this, I don't
know how.

2

The curtains opened and there was
an old man in a headdress of feathers,
leather leggings and a vest made
from the skin of some animal. He danced

in a kind of surly rapture, and the trees
in the fields far away

began to mutter and suck up their long roots.
Slowly they advanced until they stood
pressed to the schoolhouse windows.

3

I don't know
lots of things but I know this: next year
when spring
flows over the starting point I'll think I'm going to
drown in the shimmering miles of it and then
one or two birds will fly me over
the threshold.
                    As for the pain
of others, of course it tries to be
abstract, but then

there flares up out of a vanished wilderness, like fire,
still blistering: the wrinkled face
of an old Chippewa
smiling, hating us,
dancing for his life.

∽ THE SWIMMER

All winter the water
 has crashed over
  the cold sand. Now
   it breaks over the thin

branch of your body.
 You plunge down, you swim
  two or three strokes, you dream
   of lingering

in the luminous undertow
 but can't; you splash
  through the bursting
   white blossoms,

the silk sheets — gasping,
 you rise and struggle
  lightward, finding your way
   through the blue ribs back

to the sun, and emerge
 as though for the first time.
  Poor fish,
   poor flesh,

you can never forget.
 Once every wall was water,
  the soft strings filled
   with a perfect nourishment,

pumping your body full
    of appetite, elaborating
        your stubby bones, tucking in,
            like stars,

the seeds of restlessness
    that made you, finally,
        swim toward the world,
            kicking and shouting

but trailing a mossy darkness —
    a dream that would never breathe air
        and was hinged to your wildest joy
            like a shadow.

⌒ MILKWEED

The milkweed now with their many pods are standing
like a country of dry women.
The wind lifts their flat leaves and drops them.
This is not kind, but they retain a certain crisp glamour;
moreover, it's easy to believe
each one was once young and delicate, also
frightened; also capable
of a certain amount of rough joy.
I wish you would walk with me out into the world.
I wish you could see what has to happen, how
each one crackles like a blessing
over its thin children as they rush away.

∽ THE WAVES

The sea
   isn't a place
      but a fact, and
         a mystery

under its green and black
   cobbled coat that never
      stops moving.
        When death

happens on land, on some
   hairpin piece of road,
      we crawl past,
        imagining

over and over that moment
   of disaster. After the storm
      the other boats didn't
        hesitate — they spun out

from the rickety pier, the men
   bent to the nets or turning
      the weedy winches.
        Surely the sea

is the most beautiful fact
   in our universe, but
      you won't find a fisherman
        who will say so;

what they say is,
   See you later.
      Gulls white as angels scream
         as they float in the sun

just off the sterns;
   everything is here
      that you could ever imagine.
         And the bones

of the drowned fisherman
   are returned, half a year later,
      in the glittering,
         laden nets.

∾ LANDSCAPE

Isn't it plain the sheets of moss, except that
they have no tongues, could lecture
all day if they wanted about

spiritual patience? Isn't it clear
the black oaks along the path are standing
as though they were the most fragile of flowers?

Every morning I walk like this around
the pond, thinking: if the doors of my heart
ever close, I am as good as dead.

Every morning, so far, I'm alive. And now
the crows break off from the rest of the darkness
and burst up into the sky — as though

all night they had thought of what they would like
their lives to be, and imagined
their strong, thick wings.

∽ THE SHARK

The domed head rose above the water, white
as a spill of milk. It had taken the hook. It swirled,
and all they could see then was the grinding
and breaking of water, its thrashing, the teeth
in the grin and grotto of its impossible mouth.
The line they refused to cut ran down like a birth cord
into the packed and strategic muscles.
The sun shone.

It was not a large boat. The beast plunged
with all it had caught onto, deep
under the green waves — a white
retching thing, it turned
toward the open sea. And it was hours before

they came home, hauling their bloody prize,
well-gaffed. A hundred gulls followed,
picking at the red streams,
as it sang its death song of vomit and bubbles,
as the blood ran from its mouth
that had no speech to rail against this matter —

speech, that gives us all there may be of the future —
speech, that makes all the difference, we like to say.
And I say: in the wilderness of our wit
we will all cry out last words — heave and spit them
into the shattering universe someday, to someone.

Whoever He is, count on it: He won't answer.
The inventor is like the hunter — each

in the crease and spasm of the thing about to be done
is lost in his work. All else is peripheral,
remote, unfelt. The connections have broken.

Consider the evening:
the shark winched into the air; men
lifting the last bloody hammers.
And Him, somewhere, ponderously lifting another world,
setting it free to spin, if it can,
in a darkness you can't imagine.

∿ STORM IN MASSACHUSETTS, SEPTEMBER 1982

A hot day,
   a clear heaven — then
     clouds bulge
       over the horizon

and the wind turns
   like a hundred black swans
     and the first faint noise
       begins.

I think
   of my good life,
     I think
       of other lives

being blown apart
   in field after distant field.
     All over the world —
       I'm sure of it —

life is much the same
   when it's going well —
     resonant
       and unremarkable.

But who,
   not under disaster's seal,
     can understand what life is like
       when it begins to crumble?

Now the noise is bulbous,
   dense, drumming
      over the hills,
         and approaching.

So safe,
   so blank of imagination,
      so deadly of heart,
         I listen

to those dropped and rolling
   rounds of thunder.
      They only sound
         like gunfire.

～ ACID

In Jakarta,
among the venders
of flowers and soft drinks,
I saw a child
with a hideous mouth,
begging,
and I knew the wound was made
for a way to stay alive.
What I gave him
wouldn't keep a dog alive.
What he gave me
from the brown coin
of his sweating face
was a look of cunning.
I carry it
like a bead of acid
to remember how,
once in a while,
you can creep out of your own life
and become someone else —
an explosion
in that nest of wires
we call the imagination.
I will never see him
again, I suppose.
But what of this rag,
this shadow
flung like a boy's body
into the walls

of my mind, bleeding
their sour taste —
insult and anger,
the great movers?

✒ BLACK SNAKES

Suddenly
there I was
on the warm rocks — fear
like a mallet
slung against
metal — it was
that sudden,
that loud,
though in truth
there was no sound, only
the rough wing of fright
rushing
through our bodies.
One flowed
under the leaves, the other flared
half its length
into the air
against my body, then swirled
away. Once I had steadied,
I thought: how valiant!
and I wished
I had come softly, I wished
they were my dark friends.
For a moment I stared
through the impossible gates.
Then I saw them, under the vines,
coiled, cringing,

wishing me gone
with their stone eyes.
Not knowing what I would do
next, their tongues
shook like fire
at the echoes of my body —
that column of death
plunging
through the delicate woods.

∽ THE MOTHS

There's a kind of white moth, I don't know
what kind, that glimmers, it does,
in the daylight,
in mid-May
in the forest, just
as the pink moccasin flowers
are rising.

If you notice anything,
it leads you to notice
more
and more.

And anyway
I was so full of energy.
I was always running around, looking
at this and that.

If I stopped
the pain
was unbearable.

If I stopped and thought, maybe
the world
can't be saved,
the pain
was unbearable.

Finally, I had noticed enough.
All around me in the forest
the white moths floated.

How long do they live, fluttering
in and out of the shadows?

You aren't much, I said
one day to my reflection
in a green pond,
and grinned.

The wings of the moths catch the sunlight
and burn
so brightly.

At night, sometimes,
they slip between the pink lobes
of the moccasin flowers and lie there until dawn,
motionless
in those dark halls of honey.

∿ AT SEA

The haze
  has us
    in a slow, pink
      and gray

confusion; everything
  we know —
    the horizon,
      for example,

and the distant
  ridge of land —
    has vanished,
      the boat

glides without a sound
  over a sea of curled
    and luminous glass,
      there are clouds

in the sky wherever
  that is, and clouds
    in the water,
      and maybe

we have entered heaven
  already, the happy boat
    sliding
      like a bee

down the throat of a huge
   damp flower.
     Some birds,
       like streamers of white silk,

approach us, crying.
   Ah, yes,
     how easy,
       how familiar

it seems now,
   that long
     lovely thrusting up and down
       of wings.

～ 1945–1985: POEM FOR THE ANNIVERSARY

Sometimes,
walking for hours through the woods,
I don't know what I'm looking for,
maybe for something
shy and beautiful to come
frisking out of the undergrowth.

Once a fawn did just that.
My dog didn't know
what dogs usually do.
And the fawn didn't know.

As for the doe, she was probably
down in Round Pond, swizzling up
the sweet marsh grass and dreaming
that everything was fine.

～

The way I'd like to go on living in this world
wouldn't hurt anything, I'd just go on
walking uphill and downhill, looking around,
and so what if half the time I don't know
what for —

so what if it doesn't come
to a hill of beans —

so what if I vote liberal,

and am Jewish,
or Lutheran —

or a game warden —

or a bingo addict —

and smoke a pipe?

～

In the films of Dachau and Auschwitz and Bergen-Belsen
the dead rise from the earth
and are piled in front of us, the starved
stare across forty years,
and lush, green, musical Germany
shows again its iron claw, which won't

ever be forgotten, which won't
ever be understood, but which did,
slowly, for years, scrape across Europe

～

while the rest of the world
did nothing.

～

Oh, you never saw
such a good leafy place, and
everything was fine, my dog and the fawn
did a little dance,
they didn't get serious.
Then the fawn clambered away through the leaves

and my gentle dog followed me away.

～

Oh, you never saw such a garden!
A hundred kinds of flowers in bloom!
A waterfall, for pleasure and nothing else!
The garden furniture is white,
tables and chairs in the cool shade.
A man sits there, the long afternoon before him.
He is finishing lunch, some kind
of fruit, chicken, and a salad.
A bottle of wine with a thin and beaded neck.

He fills a glass.
You can tell it is real crystal.
He lifts it to his mouth and drinks peacefully.

It is the face of Mengele.

～

Later
the doe came wandering back in the twilight.
She stepped through the leaves. She hesitated,
sniffing the air.

Then she knew everything.

～

The forest grew dark.

She nuzzled her child wildly.

❧ AT LOXAHATCHIE

All day
the alligators
lumbered into and out of
the water, herons

stood in the trees
combing their white shoulders,
vultures
floating just under the clouds

were in no hurry —
sooner or later
the mysterious circles
always closed.

I had dreamed of such a place,
but this was my first visit
to the thick parks and the state of mind
called Florida. Streams

wandered everywhere
among the dense mangroves.
At one I paused
to drink, and inside me

the water whispered: *And now, like us,*
you are a million years old.
But at the same time
the enormous and waxy flowers

of the shrubs around me, whose names
I did not know,
were nodding in the wind and sighing:
Be born! And I knew

whatever my place in this garden
it was not to be what I had always been —
the gardener.
Everywhere the reptiles thrashed

while birds exploded into heavenly
hymns of rough song and the vultures
drifted like black angels and clearly nothing
needed to be saved.

∽ COMING HOME

When we're driving, in the dark,
on the long road
to Provincetown, which lies empty
for miles, when we're weary,
when the buildings
and the scrub pines lose
their familiar look,
I imagine us rising
from the speeding car,
I imagine us seeing
everything from another place — the top
of one of the pale dunes
or the deep and nameless
fields of the sea —
and what we see is the world
that cannot cherish us
but which we cherish,
and what we see is our life
moving like that,
along the dark edges
of everything — the headlights
like lanterns
sweeping the blackness —
believing in a thousand
fragile and unprovable things,
looking out for sorrow,
slowing down for happiness,
making all the right turns

right down to the thumping
barriers to the sea,
the swirling waves,
the narrow streets, the houses,
the past, the future,
the doorway that belongs
to you and me.

∽ THE SUNFLOWERS

Come with me
   into the field of sunflowers.
      Their faces are burnished disks,
      their dry spines

creak like ship masts,
   their green leaves,
      so heavy and many,
        fill all day with the sticky

sugars of the sun.
   Come with me
      to visit the sunflowers,
      they are shy

but want to be friends;
   they have wonderful stories
      of when they were young —
      the important weather,

the wandering crows.
   Don't be afraid
      to ask them questions!
      Their bright faces,

which follow the sun,
   will listen, and all
      those rows of seeds —
      each one a new life! —

hope for a deeper acquaintance;
   each of them, though it stands
      in a crowd of many,
         like a separate universe,

is lonely, the long work
   of turning their lives
      into a celebration
         is not easy. Come

and let us talk with those modest faces,
   the simple garments of leaves,
      the coarse roots in the earth
         so uprightly burning.

∾ ACKNOWLEDGMENTS

My thanks to the editors of the following magazines, in which some of these poems previously appeared.

AMICUS: *Starfish*

THE ATLANTIC: *Bowing to the Empress, A Visitor, Milkweed, Acid*

BOSTON REVIEW: *Knife*

COLUMBIA: *Driving Through the Wind River Reservation: A Poem of Black Bear*

COUNTRY JOURNAL: *At Sea, Marsh Hawks, The Chance to Love Everything*

GEORGIA REVIEW: *Dreams, At Loxahatchie, Two Kinds of Deliverance*

HARVARD MAGAZINE: *Black Snakes, Orion*

IRONWOOD: *Consequences*

KENYON REVIEW: *Poem, Rage, The Swimmer, Robert Schumann, Shadows*

MEMPHIS STATE REVIEW: *Stanley Kunitz*

PARTISAN REVIEW: *Sunrise*

POETRY: *The Moths, Banyan, The Shark*

RACCOON: *The Sunflowers*

VIRGINIA QUARTERLY REVIEW: *The River*

WESTERN HUMANITIES REVIEW: *Trilliums, Wild Geese, The Turtle, The Journey, Clamming, Morning Poem*

My thanks also to the Artists Foundation of Boston, Massachusetts, for a grant during the time I was completing this manuscript.